Fuck Off I'm Coloring

Adult Coloring Book 40 Swear Words to Color Your Anger Away

Copyright 2020 by Kr Colins

First printing 2020
ISBN 9798583623884

Ass Hole

ALWAYS
BELIEVE
IN
the
impossible

FuckYou

ALWAYS
BELIEVE
IN
the
impossible

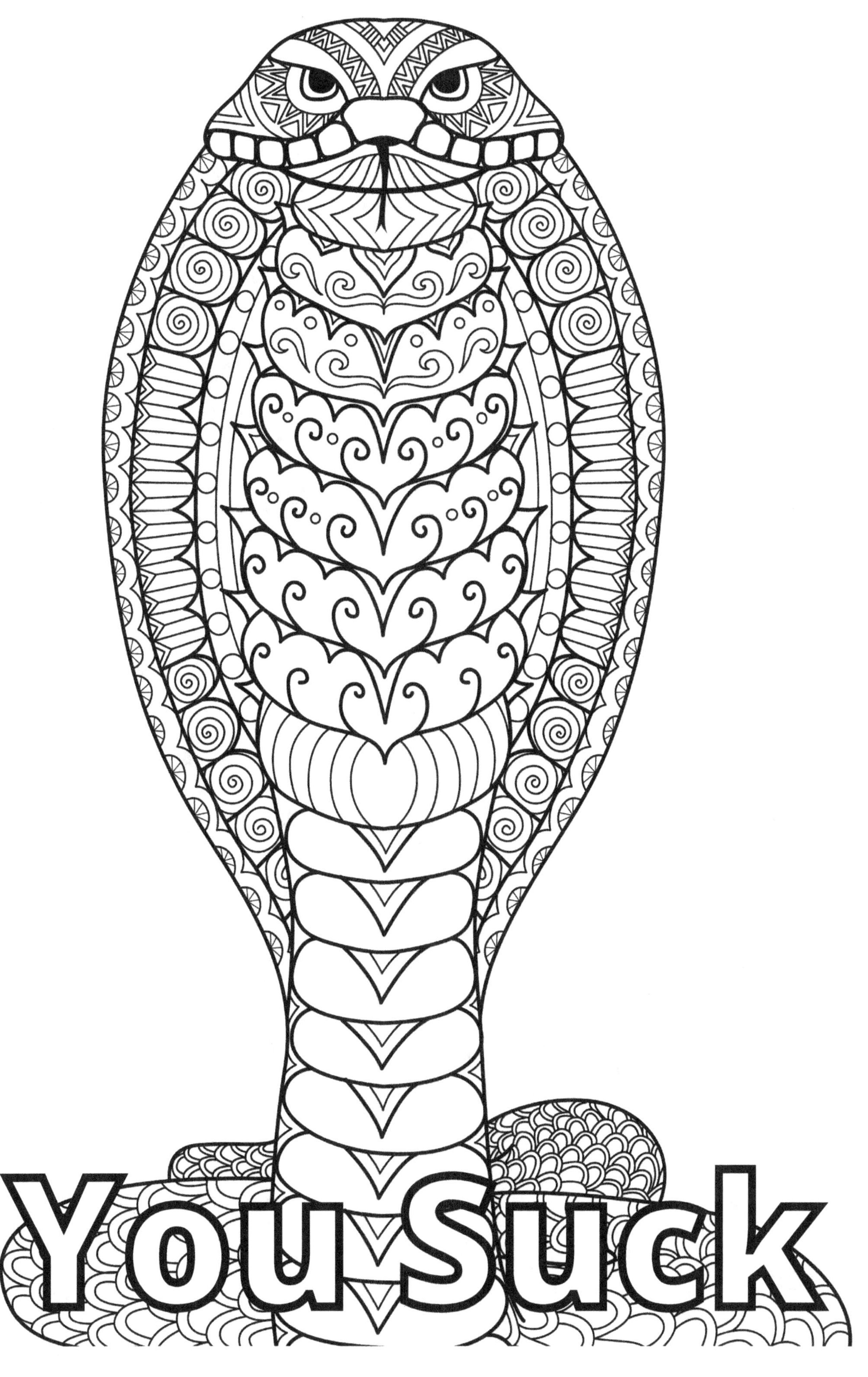
You Suck

ALWAYS
BELIEVE
IN
the
impossible

Bitch

ALWAYS BELIEVE IN the impossible

Eat Shit

ALWAYS BELIEVE IN the impossible

Piss Flaps

ALWAYS.
BELIEVE
IN
the
impossible

Idiot

ALWAYS
BELIEVE
IN the possible

Slut

ALWAYS
BELIEVE
IN
the
impossible

Cook Bag

ALWAYS
BELIEVE
IN
the
impossible

Twat

ALWAYS BELIEVE IN the impossible

Whore

ALWAYS
BELIEVE
IN
the
impossible

Wank

ALWAYS BELIEVE IN the impossible

Crap

ALWAYS BELIEVE IN the impossible

Bugger

ALWAYS
BELIEVE
IN
the
impossible

Tits

ALWAYS
BELIEVE
IN
the
impossible

Balls

ALWAYS
BELIEVE
IN
the
impossible

Prick

ALWAYS
BELIEVE
IN
the
impossible

Arse

ALWAYS. BELIEVE IN the impossible

Fart

ALWAYS
BELIEVE
IN
the
impossible

Piss

ALWAYS
BELIEVE
IN
the
impossible

Wank

ALWAYS
BELIEVE
IN
the
impossible

Cunt

ALWAYS. BELIEVE IN the impossible

Damn

ALWAYS
BELIEVE
IN
the
impossible

Bullshit

ALWAYS
BELIEVE
IN
the
impossible

Dickhead

ALWAYS
BELIEVE
IN
the
impossible

Fool

ALWAYS
BELIEVE
IN
the
impossible

Maron

ALWAYS
BELIEVE
IN
the
impossible

Goddamn

ALWAYS
BELIEVE
IN
the
impossible

Bastard

ALWAYS
BELIEVE
IN
the
impossible

Hooker

ALWAYS
BELIEVE
IN
the
impossible

Wanker

ALWAYS BELIEVE IN the impossible

Tosser

ALWAYS
BELIEVE
IN
the
*im*possible

Scumbag

ALWAYS
BELIEVE
IN
the
impossible

Cocksucker

ALWAYS
BELIEVE
IN
the
impossible

Holy Shit

ALWAYS
BELIEVE
IN
the
impossible

Oh Jesus

ALWAYS BELIEVE IN the impossible

Felch

ALWAYS
BELIEVE
IN
the
impossible

Asshat

ALWAYS
BELIEVE
IN
the
impossible

Taint

ALWAYS BELIEVE IN the impossible

Blowjob

What Do You Think About our Product?
Don't Wait and Share Your Opinion Today!

www.ingramcontent.com/pod-product-compliance
Lightning Source LLC
Chambersburg PA
CBHW081627250726
48657CB00009B/2754